The Play by
Martin Sherman

APPLAUSE
NEW YORK • LONDON

Bent: *The Play* by Martin Sherman
© 1979, 1998 by Martin Sherman

ISBN 978-1-55783-336-5

Library of Congress Catalogue Card Number 97-81187

Applause Theatre & Cinema Books
19 West 21st Street, Suite 201
New York, NY 10010
Phone: (212) 575-9265
Fax: (212) 575-9270
Email: info@applausepub.com
Internet: www.applausepub.com

Applause books are available through your local bookstore, or you may order at www.applausepub.com or call Music Dispatch at 800-637-2852

Sales & Distribution:

North America:
Hal Leonard Corp.
7777 West Bluemound Road
P.O. Box 13819
Milwaukee, WI 53213
Phone: (414) 774-3630
Fax: (414) 774-3259
Email: halinfo@halleonard.com
Internet: www.halleonard.com

Europe:
Roundhouse Publishing Ltd.
Millstone, Limers Lane
Northam, North Devon
EX 39 2RG
Phone: 01237-474474
Fax: 01237-474774
Email: roundhouse.group@ukgateway.net

BENT

for
Alan Pope and Peter Whitman

ACT I

Scene 1

The living room of an apartment. Small. Sparse furniture. A table with plants. A door on left leads to the outside hall. Nearby is an exit to the kitchen. At right, an exit to the bedroom, and nearby an exit to the bathroom.

MAX enters. He is thirty-four. He wears a bathrobe. He is very hung-over. He stares into space.

MAX: Oh God! [*Goes into bathroom—pause—then offstage, from bathroom*] Oh God!
   [MAX *returns to the living room and sits down.* RUDY *enters. He is thirty. He wears a bathrobe. He also wears glasses. He carries a cup.*]
RUDY: Here. [*Hands* MAX *the cup;* MAX *stares and doesn't take it.*] Here. Coffee!
MAX: [*Takes the cup.*] Thanks.
   [*They kiss.* MAX *sips the coffee.*]
RUDY: It's late. It's almost three. We really slept. I missed class. I hate to dance when I miss class. Bad for the muscles. And there's no place to warm up at the club. I hate that nightclub anyhow. The floor's no good. It's cement. You shouldn't dance on cement. It kills my ankle. They've covered it with wood. Last night, before the show, I pounded on the wood—real hard—and I could hear the cement. I'm going to complain. I really am. [*He goes into the kitchen.*]

7

MAX: [*Sits in silence and stares.*] Oh God.
[RUDY *returns from the kitchen with a pitcher of
water and waters the plants.*]
RUDY: The plants are dying. The light's bad in this
apartment. I wish we had a decent place. I wish
one of your deals would come through again. Oh,
listen to me, wanting a bigger place. Rosen's
gonna be knocking on our door any minute now,
you know that, wanting his rent. We're three
weeks overdue. He always comes on a Sunday.
He only cares about money. What's three weeks?
He can wait. Well, at least I got the new job. I'll
get paid on Thursday. If Greta keeps the club
open. Business stinks. Well, I guess it means I
can't complain about the cement, huh? The thing
is, I don't want to dance with a bad ankle. More
coffee?
[MAX *shakes his head yes.* RUDY *goes into the
kitchen.*
MAX *stares into space. He puts his hand on his
head and takes a deep breath, then closes his
eyes.*]
MAX: One. Two. Three. Four. Five. [*Opens his eyes,
takes another deep breath.*] Six. Seven. Eight.
Nine. Ten.
[RUDY *returns from kitchen and hands* MAX *another cup of coffee.* RUDY *resumes watering the
plants.* MAX *watches him for a moment.*]
MAX: O.K. Tell me.
RUDY: What?
MAX: You know.
RUDY: No.
MAX: Come on.
RUDY: I *don't* know. Listen, do you think I should
ask Lena for the rent money? She's such a good
person. No feeling for music, though. Which is
crazy, she's got such a good line. Perfect legs.
Teddy wants to do a dance for her in total silence.
You think that's a good idea? There's no place to

do it, though. There's no work. Lena lost that touring job. So she must be broke. So she can't lend us the money. Want some food?

MAX: Just tell me.

RUDY: What?

MAX: Must really be bad.

RUDY: What must?

MAX: That's why you won't tell me.

RUDY: Tell you what?

MAX: Don't play games.

RUDY: I'm not playing anything.

MAX: I'll hate myself, won't I? [*Silence.*] Won't I?

RUDY: I'll make some breakfast.

MAX: Was I really rotten?

RUDY: Eggs and cheese.

MAX: I don't want eggs.

RUDY: Well, we're lucky to have them. I stole them from the club. They don't need eggs. People go there to drink. And see a terrific show. Oh boy, that's funny, 'cause that show stinks. You know, I'm so embarrassed, I have to think of other things while I'm dancing. I have to think of grocery lists, they can tell, out there, that you're not thinking about straw hats or water lilies—I mean, it really shows; particularly when it's grocery lists. Your face looks real depressed, when you can't afford groceries. . . .

MAX: [*Rises and puts his hand on* RUDY's *mouth.*] Stop it. [RUDY *tries to speak.*] Stop it! [*They struggle; he keeps his hand over* RUDY's *mouth.*] I want to know what I did. [*Releases him.*]

RUDY: [*Smiles.*] I love you. [*Goes into kitchen.*]

MAX: Rudy! Your plants! I'll pull the little bastards out unless you tell me.

[RUDY *comes back in.* MAX *stands over the plants.*]

RUDY: No you won't.

MAX: Like to bet. I did last month.

RUDY: You killed one. That was mean.

MAX: I'll do it again.

RUDY: Don't touch them. You have to be nice to plants. They can hear you and everything. [*To the plants*] He's sorry. He didn't mean it. He's just hung-over.

MAX: What did I do?

[*Silence.*]

RUDY: Nothing much.

MAX: I can't remember a thing. And when I can't remember, it means . . .

RUDY: It doesn't mean anything. You drank a lot. That's all. The usual.

MAX: How'd I get this? [*Pulls his robe off his shoulder, shows a mark on his skin.*]

RUDY: What's that?

MAX: Ouch! Don't touch it.

RUDY: I want to see it.

MAX: So *look*. You don't have to touch.

RUDY: What is it?

MAX: What does it look like? A big black and blue mark. There's another one here. [*Shows a mark on his arm.*]

RUDY: Oh.

MAX: How did I get them?

RUDY: You fell.

MAX: How?

RUDY: Someone pushed you.

MAX: Who?

RUDY: Some guy.

MAX: What guy?

RUDY: Nicky's friend.

MAX: Who's Nicky?

RUDY: One of the waiters at the club.

MAX: Which one?

RUDY: The redhead.

MAX: I don't remember him.

RUDY: He's a little fat.

MAX: Why'd the guy push me?

RUDY: You asked Nicky to come home with us.

MAX: I did?

RUDY: Yeah.

MAX: But he's *fat.*

RUDY: Only a little.

MAX: A threesome with a fat person?

RUDY: Not a threesome. A twelvesome. You asked *all* the waiters. All at the same time, too. You were standing on a table, making a general offer.

MAX: Oh. Then what?

RUDY: Nicky's friend pushed you off the table.

MAX: And . . .

RUDY: You landed on the floor, on top of some guy in leather.

MAX: What was he doing on the floor?

RUDY: I don't know.

MAX: Was Greta mad?

RUDY: Greta wasn't *happy.* [*Pause.*] It was late. Most everyone was gone. And you were very drunk. People like you drunk. [*Pause.*] I'll make some food.

MAX: I don't want food. Why didn't you stop me?

RUDY: How can I stop you.

MAX: Don't let me drink.

RUDY: Oh. Sure. When you're depressed?

MAX: Was I depressed?

RUDY: Of course.

MAX: I don't remember why.

RUDY: Then drinking worked, didn't it? [*Returns to kitchen.*]

[*A blond man, in his early twenties, enters, bleary-eyed, from the bedroom. He is naked.*]

BLOND MAN: Good morning. [*He stumbles into the bathroom.*]

MAX: Rudy!

RUDY: [*Coming out of kitchen.*] What?

MAX: Who was that?

RUDY: Who was what?

MAX: *That!* That person!

RUDY: Oh. Yeah. Him. Blond?

MAX: Yes.

RUDY: And big?

MAX: Yes.

RUDY: That's the one you fell on.

MAX: The guy in leather?

RUDY: Yes. You brought him home. [*Goes into kitchen.*]

MAX: Rudy! Your plants!

RUDY: [*Returns from kitchen.*] You brought him home, that's all. He got you going. All that leather, all those chains. You called him your own little storm trooper. You insulted all his friends. They left. I don't know why they didn't beat you up, but they didn't. They left. And you brought him home.

MAX: And we had a threesome?

RUDY: Maybe the two of you had a threesome. Max, there is no such thing. You pick guys up. You think you're doing it for me, too. You're not. I don't like it. You and the other guy always end up ignoring me anyhow. Besides, last night, you and your own little storm trooper began to get rough with each other, and I know pain is very chic just now, but I don't like it, 'cause pain hurts, so I went to sleep. [*Takes* MAX's *coffee cup, pours it onto the plants.*] Here, Walter, have some coffee.

MAX: Walter?

RUDY: I'm naming the plants. They're my friends.

[RUDY *goes into the kitchen. The* BLOND MAN *comes out of the bathroom, wearing a towel. He grins at* MAX.]

MAX: Rudy!

RUDY: [*Returns from kitchen; looks at the* BLOND.] Oh. There's a bathrobe in there—in the bedroom. [*The* BLOND MAN *goes into the bedroom. A pause.*]

MAX: I'm sorry.

RUDY: It's O.K.

MAX: I'm a rotten person. Why am I so rotten? Why

do I do these things? He's gorgeous, though, isn't he? I don't remember anything. I don't remember what we did in bed. Why don't I ever remember?

RUDY: You were drunk. And high on coke.

MAX: That too?

RUDY: Yeah.

MAX: Whose coke?

RUDY: Anna's.

MAX: I don't remember.

RUDY: You made arrangements to pick up a shipment to sell.

MAX: A *shipment?*

RUDY: Yeah.

MAX: Christ! When?

RUDY: I don't know.

MAX: That can be a lot of rent money.

RUDY: Anna will remember.

MAX: Right. Hey—rent money. Maybe ... do you think ...

RUDY: What?

MAX: We can ask him.

RUDY: Who?

MAX: *Him.*

RUDY: You're kidding.

MAX: Why not?

RUDY: We don't know him.

MAX: I slept with him. I think. I wonder what it was like.

RUDY: You picked him up, one night, and you're going to ask him to loan you the rent money?

MAX: Well, you know how I am.

RUDY: Yeah.

MAX: I can talk people into things.

RUDY: *Yeah.*

MAX: I can try.

RUDY: It won't work. He thinks you're rich.

MAX: Rich?

RUDY: You told him you were rich.

MAX: Terrific.

RUDY: And Polish.

MAX: *Polish?*

RUDY: You had an accent.

[RUDY *laughs and returns to the kitchen.*
The BLOND MAN *walks out, in a short bathrobe.*
He stands and looks at MAX. *An embarrassed silence.*]

MAX: Hi.

MAN: Hi. The robe is short. I look silly.

MAX: You look O.K.

MAN: Yes? You too. [*Goes to* MAX *and kisses him, then starts to pull* MAX's *robe off, and bites* MAX *on the chest.*] Ummm . . .

MAX: Hey. Not now.

MAN: Later, then.

MAX: Yes.

MAN: In the country.

MAX: The country?

MAN: Your voice is different.

MAX: Oh?

MAN: You don't have an accent.

MAX: Only when I'm drunk.

MAN: Oh.

MAX: Last night—was it good?

MAN: What do you think?

MAX: I'm asking.

MAN: Do you have to ask?

RUDY: [*Comes in with a cup of coffee.*] Some coffee?

MAN: Yes. Thank you. [RUDY *hands him the cup. A silence.*] This place . . .

MAX: Yes?

MAN: It's really . . . [*Stops—silence.*]

MAX: Small?

MAN: Yes. Exactly.

MAX: I guess it is.

MAN: You people are strange, keeping places like

this in town. I don't meet people like you too much. But you interest me, your kind.

MAX: Listen . . .

MAN: Oh, look, it doesn't matter, who you are, who I am. I'm on vacation. *That* matters. The country will be nice.

MAX: What's the country?

MAN: The house. Your house. Your country house.

MAX: [*To* RUDY] My country house?

RUDY: Oh. That. I forgot to tell you about that. We're driving there this afternoon.

MAX: To our country house?

RUDY: *Your* country house.

MAX: How do we get there?

RUDY: Car.

MAX: Mine?

RUDY: Right.

MAX: Why don't we stay here?

MAN: Don't make jokes. You promised me two days in the country.

MAX: Your name.

MAN: Yes?

MAX: I forgot your name.

MAN: Wolf.

MAX: Wolf? Good name.

WOLF: I didn't forget yours.

MAX: Look, Wolf, I don't have a car.

WOLF: Sure you do.

MAX: No.

WOLF: You showed me. On the street. Pointed it out.

MAX: Did I? It wasn't mine.

WOLF: Not yours?

MAX: No. I don't have a house in the country, either.

WOLF: Of course you do. You told me all about it.

MAX: I was joking.

WOLF: I don't like jokes. You don't want me with you, is that it? Maybe I'm not good enough for

you. Not rich enough. My father made watches.
That's not so wonderful. Is it, Baron?
[*Pause.*]

MAX: Baron?

RUDY: Don't look at me. *That* one I didn't know
about.

MAX: Baron. [*Begins to laugh.*]
[*There is a loud knock at the front door.*]

RUDY: Rosen!

MAX: Shit!

WOLF: You like to laugh at me, Baron?
[*The knocking continues.*]

MAX: Listen, Wolf darling, you're really very sweet
and very pretty and I like you a lot, but you see,
I'm not too terrific, because I have a habit of getting drunk and stoned and grand and making
things up. Believe me, I'm not a baron. There is
no country house. There is no money. I don't
have *any* money. Sometimes I do. Sometimes I
sell cocaine, sometimes I find people to invest in
business deals, sometimes . . . well, I scrounge,
see, and I'm good at it, and in a few weeks I will
have some money again. But right now, nothing.
Rudy and I can't pay our rent. This rent. Right
here. This lousy apartment. That's all we have.
And that man knocking at our door is our landlord. And he's going to throw us out. Because we
can't pay our rent. Out into the streets, Wolf, the
streets. Filled with filth, vermin. And lice. And
. . . urine. Urine! Unless someone can help us out.
Unless someone gives us a hand. *That's* the truth.
Look, you don't believe me, I'll show you. Right
out there we have, just like in the movies, the
greedy landlord. [*Puts his hand on the door-
knob.*] Fanfare please.
[RUDY *simulates a trumpet call.*]

MAX: Here he is, the one and only, Abraham Rosen!
[MAX *swings the door open with a flourish. Two
men are standing outside—a Gestapo* CAPTAIN

and an OFFICER *in full Nazi uniform—both holding guns.* MAX *shuts the door.*]

MAX: That's not Rosen!

[*The door is kicked open. The* CAPTAIN *points to* WOLF.]

CAPTAIN: *HIM!*

WOLF: No!

[WOLF *throws the coffee cup at the* CAPTAIN *and runs into the bathroom. The* CAPTAIN *and the* OFFICER *run after him.* RUDY *starts toward the bathroom;* MAX *pulls him back.*]

MAX: Idiot! Run!

[MAX *grabs* RUDY *and they run out the front door. The lights black out on the left side of the stage. A shot rings out in the bathroom.* WOLF *screams. The lights rise on the left side of the stage, as* GRETA *enters.* GRETA *is a man dressed as a woman. He wears a silver dress, high green leather boots, and a top hat and carries a silver cane. He is both elegant and bizarre.*

The CAPTAIN *watches as the* OFFICER *drags* WOLF *out of the bathroom.* WOLF *is bleeding, but still alive. He looks up at the* CAPTAIN *and crawls slowly toward him.*]

WOLF: Bastard!

CAPTAIN: Wolfgang Granz, we have an order for your arrest. You resisted. Too bad.

[*The* CAPTAIN *grabs* WOLF *by the neck, takes out a knife, and slits his throat.*

GRETA *tugs at a rope above him and pulls down a trapeze. He thrusts himself up onto the trapeze bar and sits there.*

A projection in the center of the stage reads:
BERLIN—1934
Lights out on the apartment. Full spotlight on GRETA.]

Scene 2

GRETA *sits on the trapeze. He sings in a smoky,*
seductive voice.

GRETA: Streets of Berlin,
           I must leave you soon,
           Ah!
           Will you forget me?
           Was I ever really here?

           Find me a bar
           On the cobblestoned streets
           Where the boys are pretty.
           I cannot love
           For more than one day
           But one day is enough in this city.

           Find me a boy
           With two ocean-blue eyes
           And show him no pity.
           Take out his eyes,
           He never need see
           How they eat you alive in this city.

           Streets of Berlin,
           Will you miss me?
           Streets of Berlin,
           Do you care?
           Streets of Berlin,
           Will you cry out
           If I vanish
           Into thin air?

GRETA: [*Spotlight dims. Lights rise on* GRETA'S
    Club. The stage is to the left. GRETA'S *dressing*

room is on the right—a chair facing a mirror, and a screen to change behind. GRETA *enters the dressing room. The lights fade on the rest of his club.*] My heroes! Where are you?

[MAX *and* RUDY *come from behind the screen. They are dressed in trousers and shirts, pieces of nightclub costumes.* GRETA *looks at them.*]

GRETA: Schmucks!

[MAX *sits on a stool, lost in thought.* GRETA *sits in the chair, adjusting his costume in the mirror.*]

GRETA: I'm getting rid of all the rough songs. Who am I kidding? I'm getting rid of the club. Well— maybe. Maybe not. I'll turn it into something else. We'll see.

RUDY: Is it safe?

GRETA: What?

RUDY: For us to go home?

GRETA: You fucking queers, don't you have any brains at all? No, it's not safe.

RUDY: I want to go home.

GRETA: You can't. You can't go anyplace.

RUDY: I have to get my plants.

GRETA: Oh, Jesus! Forget your plants. You can't go home. You certainly can't stay here. And you can't contact friends, so don't try to see Lena, she's a good kid, you'll get her into a lot of trouble. You understand? You have to leave Berlin.

RUDY: Why? I live here, I work here.

GRETA: No, you don't. You're fired.

RUDY: I *don't* understand. What did we do? Why should we leave?

GRETA: Don't leave. Stay. Be *dead* schmucks. Who gives a damn? I don't.

MAX: [*Looks up.*] Who was he?

GRETA: Who was who?

MAX: The blond?

GRETA: Wolfgang Granz.

MAX: What's that mean?

GRETA: He was Karl Ernst's boyfriend.

MAX: Who's Karl Ernst?

GRETA: What kind of world do you live in? Aren't you guys ever curious about what's going on?

MAX: Greta, don't lecture. Who's Karl Ernst?

GRETA: Von Helldorf's deputy. You know Von Helldorf?

MAX: The head of the storm troopers in Berlin.

GRETA: I don't believe it. You've actually *heard* of someone. Right. Second in command at the SA, immediately under Ernst Rohm.

RUDY: Oh. Ernst Rohm. I know him. [MAX *and* GRETA *stare at him.*] He's that fat queen, with those awful scars on his face, a real big shot, friend of Hitler's, runs around with a lot of beautiful boys. Goes to all the clubs; I sat at his table once. He's been *here* too, hasn't he?

MAX: Rudy, shut up.

RUDY: Why?

MAX: Just shut up, O.K.? [*To* GRETA] So?

GRETA: So Hitler had Rohm arrested last night.

MAX: You're kidding. He's Hitler's right-hand man.

GRETA: Was. He's dead. Just about anyone who's high up in the SA is dead. Your little scene on top of that table was *not* the big event of the evening. It was a bloody night. The city's in a panic. Didn't you see the soldiers on the streets? The SS. How'd you get here in your bathrobes? Boy, you have dumb luck, that's all. The talk is that Rohm and his storm troopers—Von Helldorf, Ernst, your blond friend, the lot—were planning a coup. I don't believe it. What the hell, let them kill each other, who cares? Except, it's the end of the club. As long as Rohm was around, a queer club was still O.K. Anyhow, that's who you had, baby—Wolfgang Granz. I hope he was a good fuck. What's the difference? You picked up the wrong guy, that's all.

RUDY: We can explain to somebody. It's not like we knew him.

GRETA: Sure. Explain it all to the SS. You don't explain. Not anymore. You know, you queers are not very popular anyhow. It was just Rohm keeping you all safe. Now you're like Jews. Unloved, baby, unloved.

RUDY: How about you?

GRETA: *Me?* Everyone knows I'm not queer. I got a wife and kids. Of course, that doesn't mean much these days, does it? But—I still ain't queer! As for this . . . [*Fingers his costume.*] I go where the money is. Was.

MAX: [*Gets up.*] Money.

GRETA: Right.

MAX: Money. Ah! Greta!

GRETA: What's with you?

MAX: How much?

GRETA: How much what?

MAX: How much did they give you?

GRETA: [*Laughs.*] Oh. [*Takes out a roll of money.*] This much.

MAX: And you told them where Granz was?

GRETA: Told them, hell—I showed them your building.

RUDY: Greta, you didn't.

GRETA: Why not? You don't play games with the SS. Anyhow, it's just what he would do, your big shot here. He's into money, too. He just isn't very good at it. Me, I'm dynamite. Here. I'll do you a favor. Take it. [*Holds out the money.*]

RUDY: No.

GRETA: It will help.

RUDY: We don't want it.

MAX: Shut up, Rudy.

RUDY: Stop telling me to—

MAX: Shut up! It's not enough.

MAX: We need more.

GRETA: So get more.

MAX: If they catch us, it won't help you.

GRETA: Oh? A threat? [*Pause.*] Tell you what. I'll

do you a favor. Take some more. [*Holds out some more money.*] I've made a lot off your kind, so I'm giving a little back. Take it all.

RUDY: Don't take it.

MAX: O.K. [*Takes the money.*]

GRETA: Now get out.

MAX: [*To* RUDY] Come on . . .

RUDY: Where? I'm not leaving Berlin.

MAX: We have to.

RUDY: We don't have to.

MAX: They're looking for us.

RUDY: But I live here.

MAX: Come on. . . .

RUDY: I've paid up for dance class for the next two weeks. I can't leave. And my plants . . .

MAX: Jesus! Come on!

RUDY: If you hadn't gotten so drunk . . .

MAX: Don't.

RUDY: Why'd you have to take him home?

MAX: How do I know? *I don't remember.*

RUDY: You've ruined everything.

MAX: Right. I always do. So you go off on your own, O.K.? Go back to dance class. They can shoot you in the middle of an arabesque. Take half. [*Holds out some money.*]

RUDY: I don't want it.

MAX: Then fuck it! [*Starts to leave.*]

RUDY: Max!

GRETA: Max. He can't handle it alone. Look at him. Stick together. [MAX *turns back to* RUDY.] Take his hand, schmuck. [RUDY *takes* MAX's *hand.*] That's right.

RUDY: Where are we going to go?

GRETA: *Don't.* Don't say anything in front of me. Get out.

[MAX *stares at* GRETA. *Then he tugs at* RUDY *and pulls him out of the room.* GRETA *removes his wig. He stares at his face in the mirror, as*
BLACKOUT

Scene 3

Lights up on a park in Cologne.
*A middle-aged man, well dressed (*FREDDIE*) sits on*
a bench. He is reading a newspaper. MAX *enters.*
He sees the man and goes to the bench. The man
looks up.

FREDDIE: Sit down.

[MAX *sits.*]

FREDDIE: Pretend we're strangers. Having a little
conversation in the park. Perfectly normal. [*Folds
the newspaper.*] Do something innocent. Feed
the pigeons.

MAX: There aren't any pigeons.

FREDDIE: Here. [*Hands* MAX *an envelope.*]

MAX: You look good.

FREDDIE: You look older.

MAX: What's in this?

FREDDIE: Your papers and a ticket to Amsterdam.

MAX: Just one?

FREDDIE: Yes.

MAX: Shit.

FREDDIE: Keep your voice down. Remember, we're
strangers. Just a casual conversation. Perfectly
normal.

MAX: One ticket. I told you on the phone . . .

FREDDIE: *One* ticket. That's all.

MAX: I can't take it. Damn it, I'd kill for this. Here.
[*Gives the envelope back.*] Thanks anyway. [*Gets
up.*]

FREDDIE: Sit down. It wasn't easy getting new papers for you. If the family finds out . . .

[MAX *sits.*]

FREDDIE: I have to be careful. They've passed a
law, you know. We're not allowed to be fluffs any-

more. We're not even allowed to kiss or embrace. Or fantasize. They can arrest you for having fluff thoughts.

MAX: [*Laughs.*] Oh, Uncle Freddie.

FREDDIE: It's not funny.

MAX: It is.

FREDDIE: The family takes care of me. But you. Throwing it in everyone's face. No wonder they don't want anything to do with you. Why couldn't you have been quiet about it? Settled down, gotten married, paid for a few boys on the side. No one would have known. Ach! Take this ticket.

MAX: I can't. Stop giving it to me.

[*Silence.*]

FREDDIE: Look over there.

MAX: Where?

FREDDIE: Over there. See him?

MAX: Who?

FREDDIE: With the mustache.

MAX: Yes.

FREDDIE: Cute.

MAX: I guess.

FREDDIE: Think he's a fluff?

MAX: I don't care.

FREDDIE: You've been running for two years now. Haven't you? With that dancer. The family knows all about it. You can't live like that. Take this ticket.

MAX: I need two.

FREDDIE: I can't get two.

MAX: Of course you can.

FREDDIE: Yes. I think he is a fluff. You have to be so careful now. What is it? Do you love him?

MAX: Who?

FREDDIE: The dancer.

MAX: Jesus!

FREDDIE: Do you?

MAX: Don't be stupid. What's love? Bullshit. I'm a grown-up now. I just feel responsible.

FREDDIE: Fluffs can't afford that kind of responsibility. Why are you laughing?

MAX: That word. Fluffs. Look, do you think it's been a holiday? We've tramped right across this country; we settle in somewhere and then suddenly they're checking papers and we have to leave rather quickly; now we're living outside Cologne, in the goddamn forest! In a colony of *tents*—are you ready for that? *Me* in a tent! With hundreds of very boring unemployed people. Except most of them are *just* unemployed; they're not running from the Gestapo. I'm not cut out for this, Uncle Freddie. I was brought up to be comfortable. Like you. O.K. I've been fooling around for too long. You're right. The family and I should make up. So. How about a deal? *Two* tickets to Amsterdam. And two new sets of identity papers. Once we get to Amsterdam, I ditch him. And they can have me back.

FREDDIE: Maybe they don't want you back. It's been ten years.

MAX: They want me. It's good business. I'm an only son. [*Pause.*] Remember that marriage Father wanted to arrange? Her father had button factories, too. I just read about her in the paper; she's an eligible widow, living in Brussels. Make the arrangements again. I'll marry her. Our button factories can sleep with her button factories. It's a good deal. You know it. And eventually, when all this blows over, you can get me back to Germany. If I want a boy, I'll rent him. Like you. I'll be a discreet, quiet . . . fluff. Fair enough? It's what Father always wanted. Just get us *both* out alive.

FREDDIE: I'll have to ask your father.

MAX: Do it. Then ask him.

FREDDIE: I can't do things on my own. Not now. [*Holds out envelope.*] Just this.

MAX: I can't take it.

FREDDIE: He's looking this way. He might be the police. No. He's a fluff. He has fluff eyes. Still. You can't tell. You better leave. Just be casual. Perfectly normal. I'll ask your father.

MAX: Soon?

FREDDIE: Yes. Can I phone you?

MAX: In the *forest?*

FREDDIE: Phone me. On Friday.

[FREDDIE *puts the envelope away.* MAX *gets up.*]

MAX: You look good, Uncle Freddie.

[MAX *leaves.*

FREDDIE *picks up his newspaper, glances at it, puts it down, and turns to look again at the man with the mustache, as*
BLACKOUT

Scene 4

The forest.
In front of a tent.
RUDY *sits in front of a fire. He has some apples, cheese, and a knife. He calls back to the tent.*

RUDY: Cheese! Max!

[MAX *comes out of the tent, sits down.*]

MAX: Where'd you get cheese. Steal it?

RUDY: I don't steal. I dug a ditch.

MAX: You *what?*

RUDY: Dug a ditch. Right outside of Cologne. They're building a road. You can sign on each morning if you get there in time. They don't check your papers. It's good exercise too, for your shoulders. I'm getting nice shoulders. But my feet . . . no more dancing feet. Oh, God. Here. Have some.

MAX: I don't want to eat. You shouldn't have to dig

ditches. I want some real food, for Christ's sake. [*Takes the cheese.*] Look at this. It's lousy cheese. You don't know anything about cheese. Look at all these tents. There's no one to talk to in any of them. [*Eats a piece of cheese.*] It has no flavor.

RUDY: Then don't eat it. I'll eat it. I have apples, too.

MAX: I hate apples.

RUDY: Then starve. What did you do today, while I was ditch digging?

MAX: Nothing.

RUDY: You weren't here when I got back.

MAX: Went to town.

RUDY: Have fun?

MAX: I'm working on something.

RUDY: Really?

MAX: Yeah. A deal. [*Takes an apple.*]

RUDY: Oh. A deal. Wonderful.

MAX: I might get us new papers and tickets to Amsterdam.

RUDY: You said that in Hamburg.

MAX: It didn't work out in Hamburg.

RUDY: You said that in Stuttgart.

MAX: Are you going to recite the list?

RUDY: Why not? I'm tired of your deals. You're right. This cheese stinks. I don't want to eat it. [*Pushes the food aside.*]

MAX: You have to eat.

RUDY: Throw it out.

MAX: You get sick if you don't eat.

RUDY: So what?

MAX: O.K. Get sick.

RUDY: No. I don't want to get sick. [*Eats a piece of cheese.*] If I get sick, you'll leave me behind. You're just waiting for me to get sick.

MAX: Oh—here we go.

RUDY: You'd love it if I died.

MAX: Rudy! I just want to get us out of here. These awful tents. There's no air. We're *in* the air, but there's still no air. I can't breathe. I've got to get us across the border.

RUDY: Why don't we just cross it?

MAX: What do you mean?

RUDY: This guy on the job today was telling me it's easy to cross the border.

MAX: Oh sure it's simple. You just walk across. Of course, they shoot you.

RUDY: He said he knew spots.

MAX: Spots?

RUDY: Spots to get through. I told him to come talk to you.

MAX: *Here?*

RUDY: Yes.

MAX: I told you we don't want anyone to know we're here, or that we're trying to cross the border. Are you *that* dumb?

RUDY: I'm not dumb.

MAX: He could tell the police.

RUDY: O.K. So I *am* dumb. Why don't we try it anyway?

MAX: Because . . .

RUDY: Why?

MAX: I'm working on a deal.

RUDY: Who with?

MAX: I can't tell you. I can't talk about it before it happens. Then it won't happen. I'm superstitious.

RUDY: Then why'd you bring it up?

MAX: So you'd know that . . .

RUDY: What?

MAX: That I'm trying.

RUDY: This is crazy. We're in the middle of the jungle—

MAX: Forest.

RUDY: Jungle. I'm a dancer, not Robin Hood. I can't dance anymore. I've walked my feet away. But you don't mind. You're working on deals. You worked on deals in Berlin, you work on deals in the jungle.

MAX: Forest.

RUDY: Jungle. I want to get out of here. I could
have. I met a man in Frankfurt. You were in town
"working on a deal." He gave me a ride. He was
an old man, rich too. I could have stayed with
him. I could have got him to get me out of the
country. He really wanted me, I could tell. But
no, I had to think about you. It wasn't fair to *you*.
I'm dumb, you're right. You would have grabbed
the chance. You're just hanging around, waiting
for me to die. I think you've poisoned the cheese.

MAX: It's *your* cheese. Choke on it. Please, choke
on it. I can't tell you how much I want you to
choke on it. Christ!
[MAX *gets up*.]

RUDY: Where are you going?

MAX: I have to get out of here. I can't breathe. I'm
going for a walk.

RUDY: You can't. There's no place to walk. Just tents
and jungle.

MAX: I have a fever.

RUDY: What?

MAX: I have a fever! I'm burning up.

RUDY: It's a trick. [*Gets up, goes to him, tries to
feel his forehead.*]

MAX: [*Pulls away*.] I know. I'm lying. Get away.

RUDY: Let me feel. [*Feels* MAX's *forehead*.] You
have a fever.

MAX: It's the cheese. *You* poisoned *me*. What the
hell. I'll die in the jungle. [*Sits down again*.]

RUDY: Forest. [*Sits*.]
[*Silence*.]

MAX: Remember cocaine?

RUDY: Yes.

MAX: I'd like cocaine.

RUDY: Yes.

MAX: What would you like?

RUDY: New glasses.

MAX: What?

RUDY: My eyes have changed. I need a new pre-scription. I'd like new glasses.

MAX: In Amsterdam.

RUDY: Sure.

MAX: In *Amsterdam.* Cocaine and new glasses. Trust me. Plants. You'll have plants. Wonderful Dutch plants. And Dutch dance classes. Your feet will come back. And you won't dig ditches. You'll have to give up your new shoulders, though. And you know what? We can buy a Dutch dog. Every-one should have a dog. I don't know why we didn't have a dog in Berlin. We'll have one in Amsterdam. [*Silence.*] Trust me.

[RUDY *looks at* MAX *and smiles.
Silence.*]

RUDY: How's your fever?

MAX: Burning.

[RUDY *touches* MAX's *forehead; leaves his hand on the forehead.*]

MAX: Don't.

RUDY: I'm sorry, Max. [*Strokes his forehead.*]

MAX: Don't.

RUDY: I really love you.

MAX: DON'T. [*Pulls* RUDY's *hand away.*] If they see us . . . from the other tents . . . they're always looking . . . they could throw us out . . . for touch-ing . . . we have to be careful . . . we have to be very careful. . . .

RUDY: O.K. [*Pause—starts to sing.*]
　　　Streets of Berlin,
　　　I must leave you soon,
　　　Ah!

MAX: What are you doing?

RUDY: Singing. We're sitting around a campfire, that's when people sing. This must be the way the Hitler Youth does it. They sing old favorites, too. I'm sure they're not allowed to touch either.

MAX: Don't be so sure.

RUDY: Well, it's unfair if they can, and we can't.

[*Sings.*]
Streets of Berlin,
I must leave you soon,
Ah!
[MAX *takes* RUDY's *hand, holds it, on the ground,
where it can't be seen, and smiles.*]
MAX: Shh!
[*They laugh. They both sing.*]
MAX and RUDY: Will you forget me?
                    Was I ever really here?
VOICE: [*From the darkness*] There! That's them!
[*A bright light shines on* MAX *and* RUDY.]
ANOTHER VOICE: [*From darkness*] Maximilian Ber-
ber. Rudolf Hennings. Hands high in the air. You
are under arrest.
                    BLACKOUT

Scene 5

A train whistle is heard.

*Sound of a train running through the night. A train
whistle again.*

A circle of light comes up.

*It is a prisoner transport train. We see one small
corner. Five prisoners are in the light—two men in
civilian dress, then* RUDY *and* MAX, *then a man, in
his twenties, wearing a striped uniform, with a
pink triangle sewn onto it.*

A GUARD *walks through the circle of light. He carries a rifle.*

Silence.

RUDY: Where do you think they're taking us?
[*Silence.*
The other prisoners look away.
The GUARD *walks through the circle of light.*
Silence.]
RUDY: [*To the* PRISONER *next to him*] Did you have a trial?
[*The* PRISONER *doesn't answer.*]
MAX: Rudy!
[*Silence.*
RUDY *and* MAX *look at each other. They are both terrified.* RUDY *starts to extend his hand, then withdraws it.*
A scream is heard—off, beyond the circle. RUDY *and* MAX *look at each other, then turn away.*
Silence.
The GUARD *walks through the circle of light.*
Silence.
Another scream.
Silence.
The GUARD *walks through the circle of light.*
An SS OFFICER *enters. The circle slightly expands. The* OFFICER *looks at the prisoners one by one. He stops at* RUDY.]
OFFICER: Glasses. [*Silence.*] Give me your glasses. [RUDY *hands the* OFFICER *his glasses. The* OFFICER *examines them.*] Horn-rimmed. Intelligensia.
RUDY: What?
OFFICER: [*Smiles.*] Stand up. [*Pulls* RUDY *up.*] Step on your glasses. [RUDY *stands—petrified.*] *Step* on them. [RUDY *steps on the glasses.*] Take him.
RUDY: Max!
[RUDY *looks at* MAX. *The* GUARD *pulls* RUDY *off— out of the circle. The* OFFICER *smiles.*]
OFFICER: Glasses.
[*He kicks the glasses away.*
The OFFICER *leaves the circle of light.*

The light narrows.
MAX *stares ahead.*
The GUARD *walks through the circle of light.*
Silence.
A scream is heard—off, beyond the circle. RUDY's
scream. MAX *stiffens.*
Silence.
    RUDY *screams again.*
    MAX *moves, as if to get up.*
*The man wearing the pink triangle (*HORST*)
moves toward* MAX. *He touches him.*]
HORST: Don't.
    [*He removes his hand from* MAX *and looks straight
ahead.*
The GUARD *walks through the circle of light.*]
HORST: Don't move. You can't help him.
    [RUDY *screams.*
Silence.
The GUARD *walks through the circle of light.*]
MAX: This isn't happening.
HORST: It's happening.
MAX: Where are they taking us?
HORST: Dachau.
MAX: How you know?
HORST: I've been through transport before. They
    took me to Cologne for a propaganda film. Pink
    triangle in good health. Now it's back to Dachau.
MAX: Pink triangle? What's that?
HORST: Queer. If you're queer, that's what you
    wear. If you're a Jew, a yellow star. Political—a
    red triangle. Criminal—green. Pink's the lowest.
    [*He looks straight ahead.*
The GUARD *walks through the circle of light.*
RUDY *screams.*
MAX *starts.*]
MAX: This isn't happening. [*Silence.*] This can't be
    happening. [*Silence.*]
HORST: Listen to me. If you survive the train, you

stand a chance. Here's where they break you. You can do nothing for your friend. Nothing. If you try to help him, they will kill you. If you try to care for his wounds, they will kill you. If you even *see*—see what they do to him, *hear*—hear what they do to him—they will kill you. If you want to stay alive, he cannot exist.

[RUDY *screams.*]

MAX: It isn't happening.

[RUDY *screams.*]

HORST: He hasn't a chance. He wore glasses.

[RUDY *screams.*]

HORST: If you want to stay alive, he cannot exist.

[RUDY *screams.*]

HORST: It *is* happening.

[HORST *moves away.*
The light focuses in on MAX's *face.* RUDY *screams.*
MAX *stares ahead, mumbling to himself.*]

MAX: It isn't happening . . . it isn't happening. . . .
[*The light expands.*
The GUARD *drags* RUDY *in.* RUDY *is semiconscious. His body is bloody and mutilated. The* GUARD *holds him up. The* OFFICER *enters the circle.* MAX *looks away. The* OFFICER *looks at* MAX. MAX *is still mumbling to himself.*]

OFFICER: [*To* MAX] Who is this man?

MAX: I don't know. [*Stops mumbling, looks straight ahead.*]

OFFICER: Your friend?

[*Silence.*]

MAX: No.

[RUDY *moans.*]

OFFICER: Look at him. [MAX *stares straight ahead.*] Look! [MAX *looks at* RUDY. *The* OFFICER *hits* RUDY *on the chest.* RUDY *screams.*] Your friend?

MAX: No.

[*The* OFFICER *hits* RUDY *on the chest.* RUDY *screams.*]

OFFICER: Your friend?

MAX: No.
[*Silence.*]
OFFICER: Hit him. [MAX *stares at the* OFFICER.] Like this. [*Hits* RUDY *on the chest.* RUDY *screams.*]
OFFICER: Hit him. [MAX *doesn't move.*] Your friend? [MAX *doesn't move.*] Your friend?
MAX: No. [*Closes his eyes. Hits* RUDY *on the chest.* RUDY *screams.*]
OFFICER: Open your eyes. [MAX *opens his eyes.*] Again. [MAX *hits* RUDY *on the chest.*] Again! [MAX *hits* RUDY *again and again and again....*] Enough. [*Pushes* RUDY *down to the ground, at* MAX's *feet.*] Your friend?
MAX: No.
OFFICER: [*Smiles.*] No.
[*The* OFFICER *leaves the circle of light. The* GUARD *follows him.*
The light focuses in—on MAX's *face.*
The train is heard running through the night.
The train whistles.
RUDY *is heard—moaning—and calling* MAX's *name.*
MAX *stares ahead.*
RUDY *calls* MAX's *name. The name merges with the whistle.*
MAX *takes a deep breath.*]
MAX: One. Two. Three. Four. Five. [*Takes another deep breath.*] Six. Seven. Eight. Nine. Ten.
[RUDY *calls* MAX's *name.*
MAX *stares ahead.*
The lights dim on MAX, *almost to blackout—then, suddenly, they expand and include the three other prisoners. A morning ray of sunlight.*
RUDY *lies at* MAX's *feet.*
The GUARD *walks through the circle of light.*
Silence.
The OFFICER *comes into the circle. He looks at* MAX.]
OFFICER: Stand up. [*Stares at* MAX.] We'll see. [*To*

GUARD] Take him. [*Kicks* RUDY's *body; it rolls over—looks down at it.*] Dead.
[*The* OFFICER *leaves.*
The GUARD *pushes* MAX *with his rifle. They walk out of the light.*
The lights dim on the prisoners.]
                    BLACKOUT

Scene 6

Lights up, on one side of the stage. A large barrel is on the ground. A prisoner-foreman (KAPO) stands behind the barrel, with a huge ladle. He stirs it. The KAPO wears a green triangle on his prison uniform. Prisoners come up, one by one, with bowls in their hand, to be fed. They all wear prison uniforms.

[A PRISONER *with a yellow star enters. The* KAPO *stirs the soup.*
He fills the PRISONER's *bowl. The* PRISONER *leaves. A* PRISONER *with a red triangle enters. The* KAPO *stirs the soup.*
He fills the PRISONER's *bowl. The* PRISONER *leaves.* HORST *enters. The* KAPO *does not stir the soup.*]
HORST: Only soup. You skimmed it from the top. There's nothing in it but water. No meat, no vegetables . . . nothing.
KAPO: Take what you get.
HORST: [*Reaches for the ladle.*] Give me some meat.
KAPO: [*Pushes him back.*] Fucking queer! Take what you get!
[*Blackout.*
Lights rise on other side of the stage.

A tight little corner at the end of the barracks.
HORST *crawls in and sits huddled with his bowl.*
He drinks the soup.
MAX *enters, crawling in next to* HORST. *He carries*
a bowl. He wears the prison uniform. On it is a
yellow star.].

MAX: Hi. [HORST *looks at him; says nothing;* MAX
holds up his bowl.] Here.

HORST: Leave me alone.

MAX: I got extra. Some vegetables. Here. [*Drops*
some vegetables from his bowl into HORST's
bowl.]

HORST: Thanks. [*They eat in silence.* HORST *looks*
up. Stares at MAX's *uniform.*] Yellow star?

MAX: What?

HORST: Jew?

MAX: Oh. Yeah.

HORST: I wouldn't have figured it. [*Silence.*] I'm
sorry about your friend.

MAX: Who?

HORST: Your friend.

MAX: Oh.
[*Silence.*]

HORST: It's not very sociable in these barracks.
[*Laughs.*] Is it?

MAX: [*Points to* HORST's *pink triangle.*] How'd you
get that?

HORST: I signed a petition.

MAX: And?

HORST: That was it.

MAX: What kind of petition?

HORST: For Magnus Hirschfeld.

MAX: Oh yeah. I remember him. Berlin.

HORST: Berlin.

MAX: He wanted to . . .

HORST: Make queers legal.

MAX: Right. I remember.

HORST: Looked like he would, too, for a while. It
was quite a movement. Then the Nazis came in.

Well. I was a nurse. They said a queer couldn't be a nurse. Suppose I had to touch a patient's penis! God forbid. They said rather than be a nurse, I should be a prisoner. A more suitable occupation. So. So. That's how I got my pink triangle. How'd you get the yellow star?

MAX: I'm Jewish.

HORST: You're not Jewish, you're a queer.

[*Silence.*]

MAX: I didn't want one.

HORST: Didn't want what?

MAX: A pink triangle.

HORST: Didn't *want* one?

MAX: You told me it was the lowest. So I didn't want one.

HORST: So?

MAX: So I worked a deal.

HORST: A deal?

MAX: Sure. I'm good at that.

HORST: With the Gestapo?

MAX: Sure.

HORST: You're full of shit.

[*Silence.*]

MAX: I'm going to work a lot of deals. They can't keep us here forever. Sooner or later they'll release us. I'm only under protective custody, that's what they told me. I'm going to stay alive.

HORST: I don't doubt it.

MAX: Sure. I'm good at that.

HORST: Thanks for the vegetables. [*Starts to crawl away.*]

MAX: Where are you going?

HORST: To sleep. We get up at four in the morning. I'm on stone detail. I chop stones up. It's fun. Excuse me. . . .

MAX: Don't go.

HORST: I'm tired.

MAX: I don't have anyone to talk to.

HORST: Talk to your landsmen.

MAX: I'm not Jewish.

HORST: Then why are you wearing that?

MAX: You told me pink was the lowest.

HORST: It is, but only because the other prisoners hate us so much.

MAX: I got meat in my soup. You didn't.

HORST: Good for you.

MAX: Don't go.

HORST: Look, friendships last about twelve hours in this place. We had ours on the train. Why don't you go and bother someone else.

MAX: You didn't think I'd make it, did you? Off the train?

HORST: I wasn't sure.

MAX: I'm going to stay alive.

HORST: Yes.

MAX: Because of you. You told me how.

HORST: Yes. [*Pause.*] I did. [*Pause.*] I'm sorry.

MAX: About what?

HORST: I don't know. Your friend.

MAX: Oh. [*Silence.*] He wasn't my friend.
   [*Silence.*]

HORST: You should be wearing a pink triangle.

MAX: I made a deal.

HORST: You don't make deals here.

MAX: I did. I made a deal.

HORST: Sure. [*Starts to leave again.*]

MAX: They said if I . . . I could . . . they said . . .

HORST: What?

MAX: Nothing. [HORST *crawls past* MAX.] I could prove . . . I don't know how . . .

HORST: What? [*Stops, sits next to* MAX.]

MAX: Nothing.
   [*Silence.*]

HORST: Try. [*Silence.*] I think you better. [*Silence.*] Try to tell me.

MAX: Nothing.
   [*Silence.*]

HORST: O.K. [*Moves away.*]

MAX: I made . . . They took me . . . into that room. . . .

HORST: [*Stops.*] Where?

MAX: Into that room.

HORST: On the train?

MAX: On the train. And they said . . . prove that you're . . . and I did. . . .

HORST: Prove that you're what?

MAX: Not.

HORST: Not what?

MAX: Queer.

HORST: How?

MAX: Her.

HORST: Her?

MAX: They said, if you . . . and I did . . .

HORST: Did what?

MAX: Her. Made . . .

HORST: Made what?

MAX: Love.

HORST: Who to?

MAX: Her.

HORST: Who was she?

MAX: Only . . . maybe . . . maybe only thirteen . . . she was maybe . . . she was dead.

HORST: Oh.

MAX: Just. Just dead, minutes . . . bullet . . . in her . . . they said . . . prove that you're . . . and I did . . . prove that you're . . . lots of them, watching . . . laughing . . . drinking . . . he's a bit bent, they said, he can't . . . but I did. . . .

HORST: How?

MAX: I don't . . . I don't . . . know. I wanted . . .

HORST: To stay alive.

MAX: And there was something . . .

HORST: Something . . .

MAX: Exciting . . .

HORST: Oh God.

MAX: I hit him, you know. I kissed her. Dead lips. I killed him. Sweet lips. Angel.

HORST: God.

MAX: She was . . . like an angel . . . to save my life . . . just beginning . . . her breasts . . . just beginning . . . they said he can't . . . he's a bit bent . . .but I did . . . and I proved . . . I proved that I wasn't . . . [*Silence.*] And they enjoyed it.

HORST: Yes.

MAX: And I said, I'm not queer. And they laughed. And I said, give me a yellow star. And they said, sure, make him a Jew. He's not bent. And they laughed. They were having fun. But . . . I . . . got . . . my . . . star. . . .

HORST: [*Gently*] Oh yes.

MAX: I got my star.

HORST: Yes. [*Reaches out, touches* MAX*'s face.*]

MAX: *Don't do that!* [*Pulls away.*] You mustn't do that. For your own sake. You mustn't touch me. I'm a rotten person.

HORST: No. . . . [HORST *touches* MAX *again.* MAX *hits him.*]

MAX: Rotten.

HORST: [*Stares at* MAX.] No. [*Crawls away, and leaves.*]

MAX: [*Is alone. He takes a deep breath. He closes his eyes. He takes another deep breath. He opens his eyes.*] One. Two. Three. Four. Five. [*Takes another deep breath.*] Six. Seven. Eight. Nine. Ten.

BLACKOUT
END OF ACT I

ACT II

Scene 1

One month later.

A large fence extends across the stage. In front of the fence, on one side, lies a pile of rocks. On the other side—far over—a deep pit.

MAX is moving rocks. He carries one rock from the pile to the other side and starts a new pile. He returns and takes another rock. The rocks are carried one by one. He wears a prison uniform and hat.

A GUARD *enters with* HORST. HORST *also wears a prison uniform and hat. The* GUARD *is very officious.*

GUARD: Here. You will work here.
HORST: Yes sir.
GUARD: He'll explain.
HORST: Yes sir.
GUARD: I'm up there. [*Points off, and up.*]
HORST: Yes sir.
GUARD: I see everything.
HORST: Yes sir.
GUARD: No laying about.
HORST: No sir.
GUARD: I see everything.
HORST: Yes sir.
GUARD: [*To* MAX] You.

MAX: [*Puts down his rock.*] Yes sir.
GUARD: Tell him what to do.
MAX: Yes sir.
GUARD: No laying about.
MAX: No sir.
GUARD: I see everything.
MAX: Yes sir.
GUARD: [*To* HORST] You.
HORST: Yes sir.
GUARD: Every two hours there is a rest period.
HORST: Yes sir.
GUARD: For three minutes.
HORST: Yes sir.
GUARD: Stand at attention.
HORST: Yes sir.
GUARD: Don't move.
HORST: No sir.
GUARD: Rest.
HORST: Yes sir.
GUARD: Three minutes.
HORST: Yes sir.
GUARD: A bell rings.
HORST: Yes sir.
GUARD: [*To* MAX] You.
MAX: Yes sir.
GUARD: Explain it to him.
MAX: Yes sir.
GUARD: No laying about.
MAX: No sir.
GUARD: [*To* HORST] You.
HORST: Yes sir.
GUARD: When the bell rings.
HORST: Yes sir.
GUARD: Don't move.
HORST: No sir.
GUARD: Three minutes.
HORST: Yes sir.
GUARD: He'll explain.
HORST: Yes sir.

GUARD: [*To* MAX] You.

MAX: Yes sir.

GUARD: You're responsible.

MAX: Yes sir.

GUARD: I'm up there.

MAX: Yes sir.

GUARD: [*To* HORST] You.

HORST: Yes sir.

GUARD: I see everything.

HORST: Yes sir.

  [*The* GUARD *leaves.* HORST *watches carefully, until he is far gone.*]

HORST: We had a kid like that in school. Used to lead us in Simon Says.

MAX: O.K. I'll explain.

HORST: O.K.

MAX: Hey—we can't stand here. We have to move rocks.

HORST: Yes sir.

MAX: You see those . . .

HORST: Yes sir.

MAX: You take one rock at a time.

HORST: Yes sir.

MAX: And move it over there.

HORST: Yes sir.

MAX: And then when the entire pile is over there, you take one rock at a time, and move it back.

HORST: [*Looks at* MAX. *Silence.*] And move it back?

MAX: Yes.

HORST: We move the rocks from there to there, and then back from there to there?

MAX: Yes sir.

HORST: *Why?*

MAX: Start moving. He's watching.

  [MAX *continues to move rocks.* HORST *does the same. They do so in different rhythms, at times passing each other.*]

HORST: O.K.

MAX: It's supposed to drive us crazy.

HORST: These are heavy!

MAX: You get used to it.

HORST: What do you mean, drive us crazy?

MAX: Just that. It makes no sense. It serves no purpose. I figured it out. They do it to drive us crazy.

HORST: They probably know what they're doing.

MAX: But it doesn't work. I figured it out. It's the best job to have. That's why I got you here.

HORST: *What?* [*Puts down his rock.*]

MAX: Don't stop. Keep moving. [HORST *picks up the rock and moves it.*] A couple more things. That fence.

HORST: Yes.

MAX: It's electric. Don't touch it. You fry.

HORST: I won't touch it.

MAX: And over there—that pit.

HORST: Where?

MAX: There.

HORST: Oh yes. It smells awful.

MAX: Bodies.

HORST: In the pit.

MAX: Yes. Sometimes we have to throw them in.

HORST: Oh. Well, it will break the routine. What do you mean you got me here?

MAX: Don't walk so fast.

HORST: Why?

MAX: You'll tire yourself. Pace it. Nice and slow.

HORST: O.K. This better?

MAX: Yeah.

HORST: What do you mean you got me here?

MAX: I worked a deal.

HORST: I don't want to hear. [*Silence.*] Yes, I do. What the hell is this? You *got* me here? What right do you have—

MAX: Careful.

HORST: What?

MAX: You drop the rock.

HORST: No I'm not. I'm holding it, I'm holding it. What right do you have—

MAX: You were at the stones?

HORST: Yes.

MAX: Was it harder than this?

HORST: I guess.

MAX: People get sick?

HORST: Yes.

MAX: Die?

HORST: Yes.

MAX: Guards beat you if you didn't work hard enough?

HORST: Yes.

MAX: [*Proudly*] So?

HORST: So? So what?

MAX: So it was dangerous.

HORST: This isn't?

MAX: No. No one gets sick here. Look at all those guys moving rocks over there. [*Points off.*] They look healthier than most. No one dies. The guards don't beat you, because the work is totally non-essential. All it can do is drive you crazy.

HORST: That's all?

MAX: Yes.

HORST: Then maybe the other was better.

MAX: No, I figured it out! This is the best work in the camp, if you keep your head, if you have someone to talk to.

HORST: Ah! I see! Someone to talk to! Don't you think you should have asked me . . .

MAX: Asked you what?

HORST: If I wanted to move rocks, if I wanted to talk to you. . . .

MAX: Didn't have a chance. They moved you.

HORST: Thank heaven.

MAX: Your new barracks, is it all pink triangles?

HORST: Yes. They're arresting more queers each day; they keep pouring into the camp. Is yours all yellow stars now?

MAX: Yes.

HORST: Good. You might go all religious. There was

an old man at the stones. A rabbi. Really kind. It's not easy being kind here. He was. I thought of you.

MAX: Why?

HORST: Maybe if you knew him you could be proud of your star. You should be proud of *something*. [*Silence.*]

MAX: Don't keep looking at me. As long as they don't see us look at each other they can't tell we're talking.
[*Silence.*]

HORST: Where do the bodies come from?

MAX: What bodies?

HORST: The ones in the pit.

MAX: The fence. The hat trick.

HORST: Oh. What's that?

MAX: Sometimes a guard throws a prisoner's hat against the fence. He orders him to get the hat. If he doesn't get the hat, the guard will shoot him. If he does get the hat, he'll be electrocuted.

HORST: I'm really going to like it here. Thanks a lot.

MAX: I'm really doing you a favor.

HORST: Some favor! You just want someone to talk to so you won't go crazy. And I'm the only one who knows your secret.

MAX: What secret?

HORST: That you're a pink triangle.

MAX: No. I'm a Jew now.

HORST: You are not.

MAX: They think I am.

HORST: But it's a lie.

MAX: It's a smart lie.

HORST: You're crazy.

MAX: I thought you'd be grateful.

HORST: That's why you like this job. It can't drive you crazy. You're already there.

MAX: I spent money getting you here.

HORST: Money?

MAX: Yes. I bribed the guard.

HORST: Where'd you get money?

MAX: My uncle sent me some. First letter I ever got from him. He didn't sign it, but it had money in it.

HORST: And you bribed the guard?

MAX: Yes.

HORST: For me?

MAX: Yes.

HORST: Used *your* money?

MAX: Yes.

HORST: You'll probably never get money again.

MAX: Probably not.

HORST: You are crazy.

MAX: I thought you'd be grateful.

HORST: You should have asked me first.

MAX: How could I ask you. We're in separate barracks. Do you think it's easy to bribe a guard? It's complicated. It's dangerous. He could have turned on me. I took a risk. Do you think I didn't? I took a risk. I thought you'd be grateful.

HORST: I'm *not* grateful. I liked cutting stones. I liked that old rabbi. This is insane. Twelve hours of this a day? I'll be nuts in a week. Like you. Jesus!

MAX: I'm sorry I did it.

HORST: *You're* sorry?

MAX: You haven't figured out this camp, that's all. You don't know what's good for you. This is the best job to have.

HORST: Moving rocks back and forth for no reason. Next to a pit with dead bodies and a fence that can burn you to dust. The *best* job to have?

MAX: *Yes.* You don't understand.

HORST: I don't want to understand. I don't want to talk to you.

MAX: You have to talk to me.

HORST: Why?

MAX: I got you here to talk.

HORST: Well, tough. I don't want to talk. Move your

rocks, and I'll move mine. Just don't speak to me.
[*They both move their rocks.*
A long silence.]
MAX: I thought you'd be grateful.
BLACKOUT

Scene 2

The same. Three days later.

MAX *and* HORST *are moving rocks. It is very hot.*
Their shirts lie on the ground.

A long silence.

HORST: It's so hot.
MAX: Yes.
HORST: Burning hot.
MAX: Yes.
   [*Silence.*]
MAX: You talked to me.
HORST: Weather talk, that's all.
MAX: After three days of silence.
HORST: *Weather* talk. Everyone talks about the
   weather. [*Silence.*] Anyhow.
   [*Silence.*]
MAX: Did you say something?
HORST: No.
   [*Silence.*]
HORST: Anyhow.
MAX: Anyhow?
HORST: Anyhow. Anyhow, I'm sorry. [*Stands still.*]
   Sometimes in this place, I behave like everyone
   else—bloody awful. Cut off, mean, not human,
   I'm sorry. You were doing me a favor. This is a

good place to be. And the favor won't work unless
we talk, will it?

MAX: *Move!*

HORST: What?

MAX: Talk while you're moving. Don't stop. They
can see us.

HORST: [*Starts to move the rock again.*] It's hard to
talk when you're going one way and I'm going
the other. God, it's hot.

[*Silence.*]

HORST: Somebody died last night.

MAX: Where?

HORST: In my barracks. A moslem.

MAX: An Arab?

HORST: No. A moslem. That's what they call a dead
person who walks. You know, one of those guys
who won't eat anymore, won't talk anymore, just
wanders around waiting to really die.

MAX: I've seen them.

HORST: So one really died. In my barracks. [*Silence.*]
God, it's hot.

[*Silence.*]

MAX: We'll miss the Olympics.

HORST: The *what?*

MAX: Olympics. Next month in Berlin.

HORST: I knew there was a reason I didn't want to
be here.

MAX: Maybe they'll release us.

HORST: For the Olympics?

MAX: As a goodwill gesture. It is possible, don't you
think?

HORST: I think it's hot.

[*Silence.*]

MAX: Heard a rumor.

HORST: What?

MAX: We get sardines tonight.

HORST: I don't like sardines.

MAX: It's only a rumor.

[*Silence.*]

HORST: God, it's hot.
  [*Silence.*]
MAX: Sure is.
  [*Silence.*]
HORST: Sure is what?
  [*Silence.*]
MAX: Sure is hot.
  [*Silence.*]
HORST: Suppose . . .
  [*Silence.*]
MAX: What?
  [*Silence.*]
HORST: Suppose after all of this . . . [*Silence.*] We
  have nothing to talk about.
  [*A loud bell rings.*
  MAX *and* HORST *put down their rocks and stand
  at attention, staring straight ahead.*]
HORST: Shit! I'd rather be moving rocks than stand-
  ing in the sun. Some rest period.
MAX: It's part of their plan.
HORST: What plan?
MAX: To drive us crazy. [*Silence.*] Was I awful to
  bring you here?
HORST: No.
MAX: I was, wasn't I?
HORST: No.
MAX: I had no right. . . .
HORST: Stop it. Stop thinking how awful you are.
  Come on, don't get depressed. Smile. [*Silence.*]
  You're not smiling.
MAX: You can't see me.
HORST: I can feel you.
MAX: I wish we could look at each other.
HORST: I can feel you.
MAX: They hate it if anyone looks at each other.
HORST: I snuck a glance.
MAX: At what?
HORST: At you.
MAX: When?

HORST: Before.

MAX: Yeah?

HORST: A couple of glances. You look sexy.

MAX: Me?

HORST: Without your shirt.

MAX: No.

HORST: Come off it. You know you're sexy.

MAX: No.

HORST: Liar.

MAX: [*Smiles.*] Of course I'm a liar.

HORST: Sure.

MAX: I've always been sexy.

HORST: Uh-huh.

MAX: Since I was a kid.

HORST: Yes?

MAX: Twelve. I got into a lot of trouble when I was . . .

HORST: Twelve?

MAX: Twelve.

HORST: Your body's beautiful.

MAX: I take care of it. I exercise.

HORST: What?

MAX: At night I do push-ups and knee bends in the barracks.

HORST: After twelve hours of moving rocks?

MAX: Sure. I figured it out. You got to keep your entire body strong. By yourself. That's how you survive here. You should do it.

HORST: I don't like to exercise.

MAX: You're a nurse.

HORST: For other people, not myself.

MAX: But you have to think of survival.

HORST: Sleep. I think of sleep. That's how I survive. Or I think of nothing. [*Silence.*] That scares me. When I think of nothing. [*Silence.*]

MAX: Your body's nice, too.

HORST: It's O.K. Not great.

MAX: No, it's nice.

HORST: Not as nice as yours.

MAX: No. But it's O.K.

HORST: How do you know?

MAX: I looked. I snuck a few glances, too.

HORST: When?

MAX: All day.

HORST: Yes?

MAX: Yes.

[*Silence.*]

HORST: Listen, do you . . .

MAX: What?

HORST: Miss . . .

MAX: What?

HORST: You know.

MAX: No, I don't.

HORST: Everyone misses it.

MAX: No.

HORST: Everyone in the camp.

MAX: No.

HORST: They go crazy missing it.

MAX: No.

HORST: Come on. No one can hear us. You're not a yellow star with me, remember? Do you miss it?

MAX: I don't want . . .

HORST: What?

MAX: To miss it.

HORST: But do you?

[*Silence.*]

MAX: Yes.

HORST: Me too. [*Silence.*] We don't have to.

MAX: What?

HORST: Miss it. [*Silence.*] We're here together. We don't have to miss it.

MAX: We can't look at each other. We can't touch.

HORST: We can feel . . .

MAX: Feel what?

HORST: Each other. Without looking. Without touching. I can feel you right now. Next to me. Can you feel me?

MAX: No.

HORST: Come on. Don't be afraid. No one can hear us. Can you feel me?

MAX: Maybe.

HORST: No one's going to know. It's all right. Feel me.

MAX: Maybe.

HORST: Feel me.

MAX: It's so hot.

HORST: I'm touching you.

MAX: No.

HORST: I'm touching you.

MAX: It's burning.

HORST: I'm kissing you.

MAX: Burning.

HORST: Kissing your eyes.

MAX: Hot.

HORST: Kissing your lips.

MAX: Yes.

HORST: Mouth.

MAX: Yes.

HORST: Inside your mouth.

MAX: Yes.

HORST: Neck.

MAX: Yes.

HORST: Down . . .

MAX: Yes.

HORST: Down . . .

MAX: Yes.

HORST: Chest. My tongue . . .

MAX: Burning.

HORST: Your chest.

MAX: Your mouth.

HORST: I'm kissing your chest.

MAX: Yes.

HORST: Hard.

MAX: Yes.

HORST: Down . . .

MAX: Yes.

HORST: Down . . .

MAX: Yes.
HORST: Your cock.
MAX: Yes.
HORST: Do you feel my mouth?
MAX: Yes. Do you feel my cock?
HORST: Yes. Do you feel . . .
MAX: Do you feel . . .
HORST: Mouth.
MAX: Cock.
HORST: Cock.
MAX: Mouth.
HORST: Do you feel my cock?
MAX: Do you feel my mouth?
HORST: Yes.
MAX: Do you know what I'm doing?
HORST: Yes. Can you taste what I'm doing?
MAX: Yes.
HORST: Taste.
MAX: Feel.
HORST: Together . . .
MAX: Together . . .
HORST: Do you feel me?
MAX: I feel you.
HORST: I see you.
MAX: I feel you.
HORST: I have you.
MAX: I want you.
HORST: Do you feel me inside you?
MAX: I want you inside me.
HORST: Feel . . .
MAX: I have you inside me.
HORST: Inside . . .
MAX: Strong.
HORST: Do you feel me thrust . . .
MAX: Hold.
HORST: Stroke . . .
MAX: Strong . . .
HORST: Oh . . .
MAX: Strong . . .

HORST: Oh . . .
MAX: Strong . . .
HORST: I'm going to . . .
MAX: Strong . . .
HORST: Do you feel . . . I'm going to . . .
MAX: I feel us both.
HORST: Do you . . .
MAX: Oh yes . . .
HORST: Do you . . .
MAX: Yes. Yes.
HORST: Feel . . .
MAX: Yes. Strong . . .
HORST: Feel . . .
MAX: More . . .
HORST: Ohh . . .
MAX: Now . . .
HORST: Yes . . .
MAX: Now! [*Gasps.*] Oh! Oh! My God! [*Has orgasm.*]
HORST: Ohh! . . . Now! Ohh! . . . [*Has orgasm.*]
  [*Silence.*]
HORST: Oh.
  [*Silence.*]
HORST: Did you?
MAX: Yes. *You?*
HORST: Yes.
  [*Silence.*]
MAX: You're a good lay.
HORST: So are you.
  [*Silence.*]
MAX: It's awfully sticky.
  [*Silence.*]
HORST: Max?
MAX: What?
HORST: We did it. How about that—fucking guards, fucking camp, we did it.
MAX: Don't shout.
HORST: O.K. But I'm shouting inside. We did it. They're not going to kill us. We made love. We

were real. We were human. We made love.
They're not going to kill us.
[*Silence.*]
MAX: I never . . .
HORST: What?
MAX: Thought we'd . . .
HORST: What?
MAX: Do it in three minutes.
   [*They laugh.*
   The bell rings.]

BLACKOUT

Scene 3

The same. Two months later.

MAX *and* HORST *are at attention, wearing shirts.*

HORST: I'm going crazy. [*Silence.*] I'm going crazy.
   [*Silence.*] I'm going crazy. I dream about rocks.
   I close my eyes and I'm moving rocks. Rocks
   never end. Never end. [*Silence.*] I'm going crazy.
MAX: Think of something else.
HORST: I can't think. I've been up all night.
MAX: Up all night?
HORST: Come on, didn't you hear? Our barracks had
   to stand outside all night.
MAX: No.
HORST: Yes. We stood at attention all night long.
   Punishment.
MAX: What for?
HORST: Someone in our barracks killed himself.
MAX: A moslem?
HORST: Of course not. It doesn't mean anything if
   a moslem kills himself, but if a person who's still
   a person commits suicide, well . . . it's a kind of

defiance, isn't it? They hate that—it's an act of
free will.

MAX: I'm sorry.

HORST: Sure. Yellow star is sorry.

[*Silence.*]

MAX: Heard a rumor.

HORST: What?

MAX: Sardines tonight.

HORST: I hate sardines! I hate all food. Scraps. Sardine scraps. That's all we get anyhow. Not worth
eating. Didn't know you could have sardine
scraps. [*Silence.*] I'm going crazy.

MAX: O.K. O.K. You're going crazy. I'm sorry. It's
my fault.

HORST: What do you mean *your* fault?

MAX: For bringing you here. Because you make me
feel so guilty. And you should. This job *is* the
worst. I figured it wrong. I'm sorry.

HORST: I'm glad to be here.

MAX: Oh sure.

HORST: I am.

MAX: How can you be?

HORST: That's my secret.

[*Pause.*] [*Bell rings.* MAX *starts to move rocks.*
HORST *remains still.*]

HORST: Maybe if I closed my eyes . . .

MAX: Heard a rumor.

HORST: What? [*Starts to move rocks.*]

MAX: We may get potatoes.

HORST: When?

MAX: Tomorrow.

HORST: I don't believe it.

MAX: They said so in my barracks.

HORST: Who's they?

MAX: Some guys.

HORST: Are they cute?

MAX: Cut it out.

HORST: You should be with us, where you belong.

MAX: No. But you shouldn't be *here*.

HORST: I want to be here.

MAX: Why would you want to be here—are you crazy?

HORST: Of course I'm crazy. I'm trying to tell you I'm crazy. And I want to be here.

MAX: Why?

HORST: Because. Because I love rocks. [*Pause.*] Because I love you. [*Silence.*] I do. I love you. When I'm not dreaming about rocks, I'm dreaming about you. For the past six weeks, I've dreamed about you. It helps me get up. It helps me make sure my bed is perfectly made so I'm not punished. It helps me eat the stinking food. It helps me put up with the constant fights in the barracks. Knowing I'll see you. At least out of the corner of my eyes. In passing. It's a reason to live. So I'm glad I'm here.

[MAX *is at one pile of rocks, moving them into symmetrical piles.*]

HORST: What are you doing?

MAX: Arranging these neatly. We've gotten sloppy. They can beat you for it. [*Silence.*] Don't love me.

HORST: It makes me happy. It doesn't harm anyone. It's my secret.

MAX: Don't love me.

HORST: It's my secret. And I have a signal. No one knows it. When I rub my left eyebrow at you, like this . . . [*Rubs his left eyebrow.*] . . . it means I love you. Bet you didn't know that. I can even do it in front of the guards. No one knows. It's my secret. [*Starts to cough.*] It's cold. It was better hot. I don't like it cold.

MAX: Don't love me.

HORST: I can't help it.

MAX: I don't want anybody to love me.

HORST: That's tough.

MAX: I can't love anybody back.

HORST: Who's asking you to?

MAX: Queers aren't meant to love. I know. I thought
I loved someone once. He worked in my father's
factory. My father paid him to go away. He went.
Queers aren't meant to love. They don't want us
to. You know who loved me? That boy. That dan-
cer. I don't remember his name. But I killed him.
See—queers aren't meant to love. I'll kill you too.
Hate me. That's better. Hate me. Don't love me.
[MAX *finishes arranging the rocks. He returns to
moving the rocks.*
Silence.
HORST *starts to cough again.*]
MAX: Why are you coughing?
HORST: Because I like to.
MAX: Are you catching cold?
HORST: Probably. Up all night. In the wind.
MAX: Winter's coming.
HORST: I know. [*Silence.*] I just want to close my
eyes. . . .
MAX: Heard a rumor.
HORST: I don't care.
MAX: Don't you want to hear it?
HORST: Stuff your rumors. [*Coughs again. Slips.
Drops the rock and falls to the ground.*]
MAX: Horst! [*Puts down his rock.*]
HORST: Shit. [MAX *starts toward him.*] *Don't move!*
He's watching. The guard. Don't help me. If you
help me, they'll kill you. Get back to your rock.
Do you hear me, get back! [MAX *returns, picks
up his rock, but stands looking at* HORST; HORST
is coughing—looks up at MAX.] Move! [MAX
moves the rock.] Right. I'm O.K. I'll get up. I'll
get up. Don't ever help me. [*Pulls himself up.*]
I'm up. It's O.K. [*Picks up his rock.*] These bloody
things get heavier and heavier. [*Starts to move
the rock.*] The guard was watching. He'd kill you
if you helped me. Never notice. Never watch.
Remember? I love you. But I won't help you if

you fall. Don't you dare help me. You don't even love me, so why are you going to help? We save *ourselves*. Do you understand? Do you?

MAX: Yes. I understand.

HORST: Promise me. Come on. Promise me. We save ourselves.

MAX: O.K.

HORST: Promise me!

MAX: *YES!*

HORST: You're a fool. I don't love you anymore. It was just a passing fancy. I love myself. Poor you, you don't love anybody. [*Silence.*] It's getting cold. Winter's coming.

[*They walk, moving the rocks, in silence.*]

BLACKOUT

Scene 4

The same. Two months later.

MAX *and* HORST *are moving rocks. They wear jackets.* HORST *is slower than ever, as if dazed. He is holding the rocks with difficulty.*

HORST *has a coughing spell.*

MAX: You have a barracks leader. [HORST'*s coughing continues.*] He can get you medicine. [*Coughing continues.*] He can try to get you medicine. [*Coughing continues.*] You have to ask him. [*Coughing continues.*] You have to get help. [*Coughing continues.*] You have to stop coughing—damn it. [*The coughing spell slowly subsides.*]

HORST: It doesn't matter.

MAX: If you're nice to the kapo . . .

HORST: It doesn't matter.

MAX: Some sort of medicine.

HORST: What for? The cough? How about the hands?

MAX: I told you what to do. Exercise.

HORST: They're frostbitten.

MAX: So exercise.

HORST: It doesn't matter.

MAX: Every night, I move my fingers up and down, one at a time, for a half hour. I don't do push-ups anymore. Just fingers.

HORST: It doesn't matter.

MAX: You're losing weight.

HORST: I don't like sardines. [*Starts to cough again. It goes on for a minute, then subsides.*]

MAX: It's getting worse.

HORST: It's getting colder.

MAX: You need medicine.

HORST: Stop nagging me.

MAX: See your kapo.

HORST: He doesn't care.

MAX: Ask him.

HORST: He wants money.

MAX: Are you sure?

HORST: It doesn't matter.

MAX: I thought you cared about yourself.

HORST: You don't know anything.

MAX: I thought you loved yourself.

HORST: It's too cold.

MAX: You know what? [*Silence.*] You know what? You're turning into a moslem. I'm scared.

HORST: Who isn't.

MAX: For you.

HORST: Be scared for yourself.

MAX: Why don't you listen to me?

HORST: Moslems don't listen.

MAX: You're not a moslem.

HORST: You said I was.

MAX: I didn't mean it. You're not a moslem.

HORST: You're not a Jew.

MAX: Can't you ever forget that?

HORST: If I forget that . . . then . . . I am a moslem.
   [*The bell rings.*
   They both drop their rocks and stand at attention, side by side, looking straight ahead.]

HORST: Look, I'm just cold. My fingers are numb. I can't stop coughing. I hate food. That's all. Nothing special. Don't get upset.

MAX: I want you to care.

HORST: I would. If I was warm.

MAX: I'll warm you.

HORST: You can't.

MAX: I know how.

HORST: No. You don't.

MAX: I do. I'm terrific at it. You said so.

HORST: When?

MAX: I'm next to you.

HORST: Don't start.

MAX: I'll make love to you.

HORST: Not now.

MAX: Yes. Now.

HORST: I have a headache. I can't.

MAX: Don't joke. I'll make love to you.

HORST: No.

MAX: I'll make you warm.
   [*Pause.*]

HORST: You can't.

MAX: You'll feel the warm . . .

HORST: I can't.

MAX: You'll *feel* it.
   [*Pause.*]

HORST: In my fingers?

MAX: All over.

HORST: I can't.

MAX: I'm kissing your fingers.

HORST: They're numb.

MAX: My mouth is hot.

HORST: They're cold.

MAX: My mouth is on fire.

HORST: My fingers . . .

MAX: Are getting warm.

HORST: Are they?

MAX: They're getting warm.

HORST: I can't tell.

MAX: They're getting warm.

HORST: A little.

MAX: They're getting warm.

HORST: Yes.

MAX: My mouth is on fire. Your fingers are on fire. Your body's on fire.

HORST: Yes.

MAX: My mouth is all over you.

HORST: Yes.

MAX: My mouth is on your chest. . . .

HORST: Yes.

MAX: Kissing your chest.

HORST: Yes.

MAX: Making it warm.

HORST: Yes.

MAX: Biting your nipple.

HORST: Yes.

MAX: Biting . . . into it. . . .

HORST: Yes.

MAX: Harder . . . harder . . . harder . . .

HORST: Hold it! That hurts!

MAX: Harder . . .

HORST: No, hold it. I'm serious. You're hurting me.
   [*A pause.* MAX *catches his breath.*]

MAX: You pulled away.

HORST: Damn right.

MAX: It was exciting.

HORST: For *you* maybe. I don't try to hurt you.

MAX: I like being hurt. It's exciting.

HORST: It's not. Not when you're rough.

MAX: I'm not being rough.

HORST: Yes you are. Sometimes you are.

MAX: O.K. So what? It's exciting.

HORST: Why'd you have to spoil it? You were making me warm. Why can't you be gentle?

MAX: I am.

HORST: You're not. You try to hurt me. You make me warm, and then you hurt me. I hurt enough. I don't want to feel *more* pain. Why can't you be gentle?

MAX: I am.

HORST: No you're not. You're like them. You're like the Gestapo. You're like the guards. We stopped being gentle. I watched it, when we were on the outside. People made pain and called it love. I don't want to be like that. You don't make love to hurt.

MAX: I wanted to make you warm. That's all I wanted. I can't do anything right. I don't understand you. I used to do things right.

HORST: You still can.

MAX: People liked it when I got rough. Most. Not everybody. He didn't.

HORST: Who?

MAX: The dancer. But everyone else did. Just a little rough.

HORST: Did you like it?

MAX: I don't remember. I could never remember. I was always drunk. There was always coke. Nothing seemed to matter that much.

HORST: Some things do matter.

MAX: Not to you.

HORST: They do.

MAX: I don't understand you. All day long you've been saying nothing matters . . . your cough, your fingers. . . .

HORST: They matter.

MAX: I don't understand anything anymore.

HORST: They matter. I'm not a moslem. You're not a Jew. My fingers are cold.

MAX: I want you to be happy.

HORST: Is that true?

MAX: I think so. I don't know. [*Pause.*] Yes.

HORST: Then be gentle with me.

MAX: I don't know how.

HORST: Just hold me.

MAX: I'm afraid to hold you.

HORST: Don't be.

MAX: I'm afraid.

HORST: Don't be.

MAX: I'm going to drown.

HORST: Hold me. Please. Hold me.

MAX: O.K. I'm holding you.

HORST: Are you?

MAX: Yes. You're in my arms.

HORST: Am I?

MAX: You're here in my arms. I promise. I'm holding you. You're here. . . .

HORST: Touch me.

MAX: No.

HORST: Gently. . . .

MAX: Here.

HORST: Are you?

MAX: Yes. Touching. Softly. . . . I'm touching you softly . . . gently. . . . You're safe. . . . I'll keep you safe . . . and warm. . . . You're with me now. . . . You'll never be cold again. . . . I'm holding you now . . . safe . . . and warm. . . . As long as you're here, as long as you're with me, as long as I'm holding you, you're safe. . . .

BLACKOUT

Scene 5

The same. Three days later.

MAX *is moving rocks.* HORST *is putting the rock pile into neat order.*

HORST: The air is fresh today. Clean.

[MAX *hands* HORST *a needle and a thread as he passes the rock pile.*

HORST *starts to cough—continues coughing—then stops.*]

MAX: It sounds better.

HORST: It does.

MAX: Loosening up.

HORST: It is.

MAX: The medicine is helping.

HORST: Yes. [*Silence.*] Thank you. [*Silence.*] Why don't you tell me.

MAX: Tell you what?

HORST: How you got it.

MAX: Told you. Spoke to my barracks leader. He took me to an officer.

HORST: Which one?

MAX: Some captain. The new one.

HORST: He's rotten.

MAX: You know him?

HORST: I've heard about him. You gave him money?

MAX: Yes.

HORST: I don't believe you.

MAX: Why?

HORST: You don't have any money.

MAX: Why don't you ever believe me?

HORST: Because I can tell when you're lying. You think you're so terrific at it. You're not. Your voice changes.

MAX: It *what?*

HORST: Changes. Sounds different.

MAX: Bullshit.

[*Silence.*]

MAX: Hey . . . Guess who I saw?

HORST: Where?

MAX: In my barracks.

HORST: Marlene Dietrich.

MAX: No. My landlord. From Berlin. Rosen.

HORST: Oh.

MAX: Nice man.

HORST: I thought you hated him.

MAX: Sure, I used to think he was what I was supposed to think he was.

HORST: What was that?

MAX: A lousy Jew.

HORST: He probably thought you were a lousy queer.

MAX: Probably.

HORST: Now he thinks you're not a queer. He must be very confused. It's a shame.

MAX: It's not a shame. Don't start in. [HORST *has a coughing spell.*] You *are* taking the medicine?

HORST: [*The coughing subsides.*] Of course I am. [*Silence.*] Of course I am. Max. I'm glad you got it.

MAX: So am I.

[*Silence.*]

HORST: Wish I knew how, though.

MAX: I told you.

HORST: You're a liar.

[*Silence.*]

MAX: I never met anyone like you. Can't make you believe anything.

HORST: How'd you get it?

MAX: Won't just be grateful.

HORST: Am I ever?

MAX: Suppose you don't like the answer.

HORST: I'll chance it.

MAX: Then when I tell you, you'll nag me about *that*.

HORST: You chance it.

MAX: I went down on him.

HORST: What?

MAX: I told you you wouldn't like it.

HORST: That SS captain?

MAX: Uh-huh.

HORST: He's the worst bastard in the—

MAX: I know.

HORST: You went down on him?

MAX: I had to. I didn't have any money.

HORST: You touched him?

MAX: No. I just went down on him. That's what he wanted. And I needed the medicine.

HORST: I'd rather cough.

MAX: No you wouldn't.

HORST: Is he queer?

MAX: Who knows? Just horny maybe. Sure, he could be queer. You don't like to think about that, do you? You don't want *them* to be queer.
[*Silence.*]

HORST: I guess not. Well . . . what the hell. There *are* queer Nazis. And queer saints. And queer mediocrities. Just people. I really believe that. That's why I signed Hirschfeld's petition. That's why I ended up here. That's why I'm wearing this triangle. That's why you should be wearing it.

MAX: Do you think that SS bastard would let a queer go down on him? Of course not. He'd kill me if he knew I was queer. My yellow star got your medicine.

HORST: Who needs it?

MAX: Then give it back. Throw it away. Throw it away, why don't you? And die. I'm tired of being told I should have a pink triangle.

HORST: He remember you?

MAX: Who?

HORST: Rosen?

MAX: Yes. He said I owed him rent.

HORST: What's Berlin like? Did he say?

MAX: Worse.

HORST: I miss it.

MAX: Yes. [*Pause.*]

MAX: Greta's Club?

HORST: No.

MAX: Good. You had taste. The White Mouse?

HORST: Sometimes.

MAX: Surprised you never saw me.

HORST: What were you wearing?

MAX: Things that came off. I was conspicuous.

HORST: Why?

MAX: Because I was always making a fool of myself. Did you sunbathe?

HORST: I loved to sunbathe.

MAX: By the river.

HORST: Sure.

MAX: And you *never* saw me?

HORST: Well, actually, I did. I saw you by the river. You were making a fool of yourself. And I said, someday I'll be at Dachau with that man, moving rocks.

MAX: I didn't like Berlin. Always scared. But I like it now. I miss it.

HORST: [*Finishes straightening the rocks and resumes moving the rocks.*] We'll go back someday.

MAX: When we get out of here?

HORST: Yes.

MAX: We will, won't we?

HORST: We have to. Don't we?

MAX: Yes. Horst?

HORST: What?

MAX: We can go back together.

[*An SS* CAPTAIN *enters. The* GUARD *is with him.* MAX *and* HORST *look up for a second, then continue with their task.*

The CAPTAIN *stares at* MAX *for a long time, then* HORST, *then* MAX *again.*]

CAPTAIN: [*To* MAX] You. Jew.

MAX: [*Stands still.*] Yes sir?

CAPTAIN: Feeling better?

MAX: Sir?

CAPTAIN: Your cold?

MAX: Yes sir.

CAPTAIN: Remarkable.

MAX: Yes sir.

CAPTAIN: You seem so strong.

MAX: Yes sir.

CAPTAIN: Not sick at all.

MAX: No sir.

CAPTAIN: No?

MAX: Not now, sir.

CAPTAIN: Carry on.

> [MAX *resumes moving rocks. The* CAPTAIN
> *watches* MAX *and* HORST. *He paces up and down.*
> MAX *and* HORST *move the rocks. The* CAPTAIN
> *paces.* HORST *coughs. He catches himself and
> tries to stifle it.*]

CAPTAIN: Ah. [HORST *stops the cough.*] You. Pervert.

HORST: [*Stiffens, stands still.*] Yes sir?

CAPTAIN: Are you ill?

HORST: No sir.

CAPTAIN: You have a cough.

HORST: No sir.

CAPTAIN: I heard you cough.

HORST: Yes sir.

CAPTAIN: Some thing caught in your throat?

HORST: Yes sir.

CAPTAIN: From breakfast?

HORST: Yes sir.

CAPTAIN: Ah. Carry on.

> [HORST *resumes his work.* MAX *and* HORST *move
> the rocks. The* CAPTAIN *stands watching them.
> He takes out a cigarette. The* GUARD *lights it. The*
> CAPTAIN *smokes the cigarette and watches* MAX
> *and* HORST.
>
> MAX *and* HORST *continue moving rocks.* HORST
> *coughs again, attempting to strangle it, but the
> cough comes through.*]

CAPTAIN: You. Pervert.

HORST: [*Stands still.*] Yes sir.

CAPTAIN: You coughed.

HORST: Yes sir.

CAPTAIN: You're not well.

HORST: I am, sir.

CAPTAIN: I see. [*To* MAX] You. Jew.

MAX: [*Stands still.*] Yes sir.

CAPTAIN: Watch.

MAX: Watch, sir?

CAPTAIN: Yes. Watch. [*To* HORST] You.

HORST: Yes sir.

CAPTAIN: Put down that rock.

HORST: Yes sir. [*Puts down the rock.*]

CAPTAIN: Good. Now take off your hat.
[*A long pause.*]

HORST: My hat, sir?

CAPTAIN: Yes. Your hat.

HORST: My hat, sir?

CAPTAIN: Your hat.

HORST: Yes sir.
[HORST *removes his hat.* MAX's *hand moves.* HORST *shoots him a warning stare.*]

CAPTAIN: [*To* MAX] You.

MAX: Yes sir.

CAPTAIN: Relax.

MAX: Yes sir.

CAPTAIN: And watch.

MAX: Yes sir.

CAPTAIN: [*To* HORST] You.

HORST: Yes sir.

CAPTAIN: Throw your hat away. [HORST *flings his hat on the ground.*] Not there.

HORST: Not there, sir?

CAPTAIN: No. Pick it up.

HORST: Yes sir. [*Picks up his hat.*]

CAPTAIN: Throw it on the fence.

HORST: The fence, sir?

CAPTAIN: The fence. [HORST *starts to cough.*] That's all right. We'll wait. [*The cough subsides.*] Are you better?

HORST: Yes sir.

CAPTAIN: Nasty cough.

HORST: Yes sir.

CAPTAIN: On the fence. Now.

HORST: On the fence. Yes sir.

[HORST *glances at* MAX, *another warning stare, then throws his hat on the fence. The fence sparks.*]

CAPTAIN: [*To* MAX] You.

MAX: Yes sir.

CAPTAIN: Are you watching?

MAX: Yes sir.

CAPTAIN: Good. [*To* HORST] You.

HORST: Yes sir.

CAPTAIN: Get your hat.

[*The* CAPTAIN *motions to the* GUARD. *The* GUARD *points his rifle at* HORST.]

HORST: Now, sir?

CAPTAIN: Now.

HORST: Are you sure, sir?

CAPTAIN: Quite.

HORST: Could I do without my hat, sir?

CAPTAIN: No.

HORST: [*Is silent for a moment. Feels* MAX *watching and gives him another quick glance, his eyes saying, don't move. Turns to the* CAPTAIN.] Yes sir.

[HORST *looks at* MAX. *He takes his hand and rubs his left eyebrow.*

He turns and stares at the CAPTAIN. *The* CAPTAIN *waits. The* GUARD *is pointing his rifle.*

HORST *turns toward the fence. He starts to walk very slowly to his hat. He almost reaches the fence, when, suddenly—*

He turns and rushes at the CAPTAIN. *He screams in fury.*

The GUARD *shoots* HORST. HORST *continues to lunge at the* CAPTAIN. *His hand is out. He scratches the* CAPTAIN's *face.*

The GUARD *shoots* HORST *in the back. He falls, dead.*

Silence.

The CAPTAIN *holds his face.*]

CAPTAIN: He scratched me. [*To* MAX] You. Jew. [MAX *is silent.*] You!

MAX: Yes sir.

CAPTAIN: I hope the medicine helped. [*Turns to leave, turns back.*] Get rid of the body. [*Silence.*]

MAX: Yes sir.

[*The* CAPTAIN *leaves. The* GUARD *points the rifle at* MAX, *lowers it, then walks off, after the* CAPTAIN.

MAX *stares at* HORST.

Silence.

MAX *opens his mouth to cry out. He can't.*

Silence.

MAX *walks to* HORST's *body. He tries to lift it. It is heavy. He manages to pull the body partly up,* HORST's *head resting against* MAX's *chest. He looks away. He takes* HORST, *feet dragging on the ground, toward the pit.*

The bell rings.]

MAX: No! [*He looks up—off—at the* GUARD, *then back at* HORST. *He stands at attention.* HORST *starts to fall.* MAX *pulls him up. He stands still, staring in front of him, holding on to* HORST.] It's O.K. I won't drop you. I'll hold you. If I stand at attention, I can hold you. They'll let me hold you. I won't let you down. [*Silence.*] I never held you before. [*Silence.*] You don't have to worry about the rocks. I'll do yours, too. I'll move twice as many each day. I'll do yours, too. You don't have to worry about them. [*Silence.*] You know what? [*Silence.*] Horst? [*Silence.*] You know what? [*Silence.*] I think . . . [*Silence.*] I think I love you. [*Silence.*] Shh! Don't tell anyone. I think I loved . . . I can't remember his name. A dancer. I think I loved him, too. Don't be jealous. I think I loved . . . some boy a long time ago. In my father's factory. Hans. That was his name. But the dancer. I don't remember. [*Silence.*] I love you. [*Silence.*]

What's wrong with that? [*Silence.*] What's wrong
with that?
[*He starts to cry.*
The bell rings.
He drags HORST's *body to the pit. He throws it*
in the pit.
He turns and looks at the rocks. He takes a deep
breath.
He walks over the rocks and picks one up. He
moves it across to the other side. He takes an-
other deep breath. He stands still.]

MAX: One. Two. Three. Four. Five. [*Takes another*
deep breath.] Six. Seven. Eight. Nine. Ten.
[*He picks up a rock. He moves it across to the*
other side.
He moves another rock.
He moves another rock.
He moves another rock.
He pauses. He takes a deep breath.
He moves another rock.
He moves another rock.
He stops. He tries to take another deep breath.
He can't. His hand is trembling. He steadies his
hand. He picks up another rock and starts to
move it.
He stops. He drops the rock. He moves toward
the pit.
He jumps into the pit.
He disappears.
A long pause.
MAX *climbs out of the pit.* MAX *holds* HORST's
jacket with the pink triangle on it. Puts the jacket
on.
MAX *turns and looks at the fence.*
MAX *walks into the fence.*
The fence lights up. It grows brighter and
brighter, until the light consumes the stage.
And blinds the audience.]

END OF ACT II

BACKGROUND INFORMATION

Events leading to the Nazi persecution of homosexuals and the atrocities of the concentration camps

1871 King Wilhelm established the Second Reich and adopted the Bavarian code. Paragraph 175 of this code outlawed "lewd and unnatural behaviour", prescribing prison sentences ranging from one day to five years.

1897 Adolf Brand, Magnus Hirschfeld and Max Spohr established the first Gay Rights organization—the Scientific Humanitarian Committee.

1898 A petition of 900 signatures was submitted to the Reichstag demanding the repeal of Paragraph 175. The petition failed. More petitions were submitted throughout the next ten years.

1910 The Government proposed outlawing Lesbian acts.
The bill failed to pass.

1919 Hirschfeld opened the Institute for Sexual Science in Berlin.

1920 Hirschfeld (Jewish as well as homosexual)

was attacked by Anti-Semites in Munich.
Later in the same year he was attacked by
Nazis and left on the pavement with a frac-
tured skull.

1921 Eros Theatre, the first homosexual theatre,
was started by Bruno Mattusek in Berlin. The
SA, Storm troopers, the original Nazi para-
military organization was founded.

1923 Fascists shot and wounded several members
of an audience for Hirschfeld's first pro-
homosexual film "Different from the Others"
in Vienna.

1925 Reconstruction of the National Socialist
Workers Party (the official title of the Nazi
party).
Summer: Formation of the first SS units.
Ernst Röhm, one of Adolf Hitler's chief ad-
visers, and a homosexual, pressed charges
against a 17 year old hustler who had robbed
him the 'morning after'.

1928 The National Socialist Party issued their official view of homosexuals on May 14th:
"It is not necessary that you and I live, but it
is necessary that the German people live. And
it can live if it can fight, for life means fight-
ing. And it can only fight if it maintains its
masculinity. It can only maintain its masculinity if it exercises discipline, especially in
the matters of love. Free love and deviance
are undisciplined. Therefore, we reject you,
as we reject anything which hurts our people.
Anyone who even thinks of homosexual love
is our enemy."

Reichstag Committee, by a vote of 15 to 13,

approved the Penal Reform Bill which abolished all homosexual crimes.

1929 The Stock Market crashed.
Penal Reform Bill set aside before taking effect.
The Nazis were swept to power.

1930 Ernst Röhm made head of Storm troopers.

1933 *January*: Hitler becomes Reich Chancellor
March: Dachau concentration camp set up.
April: Formation of the Gestapo (secret state police), Berlin. Hirschfeld's Institute of Sexual Science ransacked by Nazis.

1934 *June: The Night of the Long Knives*: Röhm shot dead. Hitler issued an order to purge all homosexuals from the Army, 200 SA leaders were rounded up in Berlin and massacred.
July: Gay Rights activist Kurt Hiller was arrested and sent to Oranienburg concentration camp.

A law was passed condoning the sterilization of all homosexuals, schizophrenics, epileptics, drug addicts, hysterics and those born blind or malformed. By 1935, 56,000 people had been thus 'treated'. In actual practice, the homosexuals were literally castrated rather than sterilized. All activities of Hirschfeld's League of Human Rights were banned, and the homosexual movement was crushed.

1935 On the first anniversary of the Röhm Putsch, Paragraph 175 was revised: ten possible homosexual 'acts' were punishable, including a kiss, an embrace and even homosexual fantasies.

1936 Excerpt from the speech by Heinrich Himmler: "In our judgment of homosexuality—a symptom of degeneracy which could destroy our race—we must return to the guiding Nordic principles 'extermination of degenerates' " "Protective custody"—internment in concentration camps—begins for civilian offenders, including homosexuals. The early concentration camps were detention centers: they were turned into extermination camps after 1940.

It is estimated that between a quarter and half a million homosexuals died in the concentration camps. The exact figure is not known because the Allies retained Paragraph 175a as a functioning law. A pink triangle surviving the war could not reveal why he had been incarcerated—it was still against the law and he could be returned to prison. The law was abolished in 1969, but the courts ruled that imprisoned homosexuals were still to be considered criminal and not political inmates, and thus were not entitled to restitution.